Sebastian

A BOOK ABOUT BACH

Jeanette Winter

BROWNDEER PRESS
HARCOURT BRACE & COMPANY
San Diego   New York   London

Browndeer Press is a registered trademark of Harcourt Brace & Company.

Library of Congress Cataloging-in-Publication Data
Winter, Jeanette.
Sebastian: a book about Bach/written and illustrated by Jeanette Winter.
p.   cm.
"Browndeer Press."
Summary: Describes how Johann Sebastian Bach survived the sorrows of his
childhood and composed the music the world has come to love.
ISBN 0-15-200629-X
1. Bach, Johann Sebastian, 1685-1750—Juvenile literature.
2. Composers—Germany—Biography—Juvenile literature.
[1. Bach, Johann Sebastian, 1685-1750. 2. Composers.] I. Title.
ML3930.B2W63   1999
780'.92
[B]—dc21   98-5543

First edition

A C E F D B

Printed in Singapore

The illustrations in this book were done in acrylics on
Arches watercolor paper.
The display type was set in Poetica.
The text type was set in Kennerly.
Color separations by United Graphic Pte. Ltd., Singapore
Printed and bound by Tien Wah Press, Singapore
This book was printed on totally chlorine-free Nymolla Matte Art paper.
Production supervision by Stanley Redfern and Pascha Gerlinger
Designed by Kaelin Chappell and Jeanette Winter

The first Voyager spacecraft was launched in 1977.
On the spacecraft there is a recording of sounds from Earth.
Should the spacecraft encounter any life beyond our galaxy,
the first sound that will be heard is the music of
Johann Sebastian Bach.

In the days of castles and kings,
the birds listened
when Vitus Bach played his cittern.

Vitus taught his son Hans to play the violin.
And Hans taught his son Christoph to play the violin.
Then Christoph taught his son Ambrosius to play the violin.

And when Ambrosius's son Sebastian was born,
the birds sang a welcome.

The musical Bachs came from far and wide to greet Sebastian.
Fiddles played, voices sang out.
The birds listened—
even the duke in the palace on the hill listened.

Ambrosius taught his son Sebastian to play the violin.
All the Bachs played music.

When Sebastian was nine, the music stopped.
First his mama, then his papa, died.
Sebastian was an orphan.
He went off to live with his older brother, Christoph.
Even the birds' songs could not cheer Sebastian.

But when Christoph taught his little brother
to play the clavichord,
the music sounded again.

Sebastian practiced from morning till night.
By moonlight, he copied music
to play the next day.
It was a good way to learn,
and he wanted to learn everything.

So when Sebastian was fifteen,
he set off for boarding school—on foot—
two hundred miles away.

Sebastian walked and walked and walked.
He slept in haylofts,
played for pennies in taverns,
and played for himself in the starlight.

Away at school, Sebastian learned to play the organ.
From the start, Sebastian loved this instrument—
his feet playing the pedals, his hands on the keyboard,
pulling the stops, and above all—
the mighty sound that roared from the pipes.

Sebastian walked miles to hear other organists play.
Back and forth across the land,
from one church to the next, he walked,
the sound of organ pipes ringing in his ears.

So it went at school—
playing organ, violin, harpsichord, and singing in the choir.
Then one day, Sebastian put on a wig
(for young men did that in those days),
and left school to make his way in the world.

From one church to another,
from one palace to another,
Sebastian played music—
but now it was his *own* music.

Sebastian heard the music in his head.
The melodies came fast—
as his pen raced over the page,
he rarely changed a note.

He heard one melody for the violin,
one for the trumpet,
one for the flute,
and one for the oboe.

Each instrument had its own voice.
And when all the voices sounded at the same time,
it was like good friends talking together.

Sebastian nodded to the flute, tapped his foot to the trumpet,
lifted a finger to the violin—
helping the instruments play together,
all the while playing his own part, too.
The music he heard in his head came to life all around him.

Sebastian played his music
for princes and dukes in their palaces.
But sometimes it was a hard life.

Once, a duke locked Sebastian in a jail cell for one long month—
because he had not asked permission to change jobs.
(Rulers did that in those days.)
Even as Sebastian sat behind bars,
he heard his own music, and wrote it down.

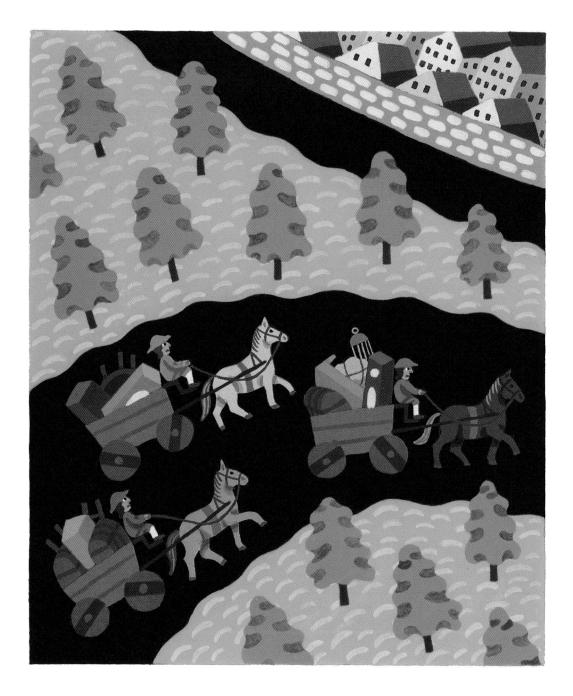

The years passed.
Sebastian became a loving husband to Anna Magdalena,
and a proud papa—of twenty children!

More and more wagons and carriages were needed
to move the Bach family from town to town.
Finally the growing family settled down
behind the walls of the city of Leipzig.

The Bachs lived in a big house
close by the big church
where Sebastian was music director.

The Bachs shared the big house
with students at the church school
where Sebastian was choirmaster.

Sebastian worked hard to provide for his family.
His days were spent teaching
unruly boys their music and Latin,
and his nights composing music
for the Sunday services—five hours long!

Every Sunday morning Sebastian's music filled the church.
But even his stern glance
could not still fidgety choirboys
during the long morning service.

The Bach house was as busy as a beehive.
There were instruments everywhere!—
under tables, on top of chairs—
with hardly a place for a visitor to sit down.

Anna Magdalena treasured the notebook Sebastian made for her,
filled with his music and poems.
At night, after the last goblet had been washed,
the whole family played music from Anna's notebook.

When the moon was high in the sky
and all the children asleep,
new music filled Sebastian's head.
He wrote and wrote until the candles burned low
as the sun came up.

Before the city was awake,
Sebastian went to the organ and played his new music.
His hands and feet flew over the keys and pedals.
The music filled the church like thunder.
Angels listened.

And kings and queens listened.

Sebastian's music echoed in the streets of Leipzig.

As Sebastian grew old, the light faded from his eyes,
until he could not see.
But still the music kept coming.
He composed one last piece
as he took his final breath.

Now Sebastian sings in the choir of angels.
And listens as his music fills the world—
across the mountains and valleys and oceans,

and into the heavens,

and maybe even far out beyond the farthest star.

Johann Sebastian Bach

was born in Eisenach, Germany, in 1685.
He lived and worked in Germany all his life,
never traveling more than two hundred miles
from his home. Bach was such a prolific composer
that were someone to copy by hand all his
compositions—over one thousand—it would take
that person forty years to complete the task.

Bach died in Leipzig, Germany, in 1750.